RUBENS

By CLAUDIA LYN CAHAN

AVENEL BOOKS

NEW YORK

Rubens © MCMLXXX by Fabbri Editori, Milan, Italy
All Rights Reserved
First U.S. Edition published 1980 by Avenel Books
distributed by Crown Publishers Inc.
Printed in Italy by Fabbri Editori, Milan.
a   b   c   d   e   f   g   h   i

Library of Congress Cataloging in Publication Data
Rubens, Peter Paul, Sir, 1577-1640.
Rubens.
1. Rubens, Peter Paul, Sir, 1577-1640—Catalogs.
I. Cahan, Claudia Lyn.
ND673.R9A4 1979a 759.9493 79-21777
ISBN 0-517-30374-4

The exceptional assimilation of the Renaissance ideals of beauty and classical form

Peter Paul Rubens, a child of the Renaissance, was the most influential Flemish artist of the seventeenth century. He was a man of action whose energy directed him toward a life of prolific painting and engraving, and later into an important diplomatic career. With his natural feeling for light and color and his exceptional assimilation of the Renaissance ideals of beauty and classical form, Rubens firmly transplanted the Baroque into northern Europe.

Peter Paul Rubens was born in 1577, into a respectable and traditional family of traders who lived in the great commercial city of Antwerp in Flanders, and he began drawing as a child. Painting was considered a valuable occupation in the late sixteenth and early seventeenth centuries, for to be an artist was honorable and useful. Art was a means of recording history, immortalizing the important political figures of the day, and expressing religious inspiration and devotion.

At age fourteen, Rubens had his first painting lessons with Tobias Verhaecht, a well-known landscape painter. In all, there were three different Flemish masters with whom he studied, and each one had something of value to teach him. His second teacher, Van Noort, taught him the lessons of naturalism – or how to paint as faithfully as possible everything the eye could see – and the various ways that color could be handled. Otto van Veen, his third teacher, instilled in him the spirit of the Italian masters of the High Renaissance.

In May of 1600, Rubens left for Italy, since no artistic education was considered complete without a visit to Rome and Venice. He spent the ensuing eight years in the service of the Duke of Mantua. During that time, he had ample opportunity to study the works of Titian, Veronese, and Tintoretto, all of whom became vital influences in his painting.

The great masters of the Italian Renaissance were, above all else, decorators. Their compositions were the perfect models of harmony, order, grace, and beauty. Florence and Rome were the homes of classical antiquity, while Venice held some of the most magnificent as well as the most sensual art of the Renaissance. During his years in Italy, Rubens acquired an understanding of

Hélène Fourment - Rotterdam, Boymans-van Beuningen Museum

classical and Renaissance ideals that was unparalelled by any other northern painter of the Baroque.

The Flemish school was instinctively naturalistic. Traditionally, the Flemish passionately admired life and were concerned with the accurate rendition of all of its characteristics. Northern painters worked with colors in oil, which they thought made the best medium for reproducing nature.

Rubens, who remained essentially a Flemish artist, took from the Italian school only that which was valuable to him and rejected the rest. From Caravaggio, he took and adapted vigorous contrasts of light and dark. He copied the powerful figures of Raphael and Michelangelo. He studied and was affected by Titian's female nudes. Tintoretto's methods encouraged him to give freedom to his brush, so that he could add aggressiveness to his gestures and speed to his movements.

In the seventeenth century, artists made their drawings from sculptures and casts. This practice stemmed from the authority that classical sculpture had gained during the High Renaissance. Rubens preferred to sketch from live models. He did not replicate nature but borrowed elements of reality which he combined with fictional themes to make the final illusion seem real.

When he returned from Italy in 1608, he was named painter to the court of the Spanish regent in the Catholic Low Countries. He moved into a luxurious home in Antwerp where he surrounded himself with the many things he loved, such as his grand art collection and a library of books reflecting his varied interests in natural history, botany, physics, geography, religion, philosophy, and law. He also kept animals, which appear in his paintings – horses, peacocks, and dogs. He soon set up his studio, and following the custom of the Italian Renaissance masters, he organized apprentices to work under his direction. There were so many pupils who wished to study in his atelier that he had to turn a large number of them away.

Rubens perpetuated the Baroque ideal of illusionism, and the use of color, light, and movement in his works. He elicited emotional response in the viewer partially through his strong use of color. His colors reflect light, thus achieving luminosity. So it was that

5

flesh, under his brush, became almost transparent, suggesting the colors of life behind it. Broad splashes of red also appear in most of his works, bearing vivid testimony to the manner in which his colors transmit emotions. The unusual positions and captured motion of his figures give his canvases life and activity, almost as if they are scenes from the theater, momentarily stopped in the midst of the drama. These techniques were strong factors in making Rubens a master of narrative and episodic painting. He could portray events, mythology, and biblical history in a manner that was both convincing and moving.

A man of intellectual curiosity, Rubens often used literature as a stimulus to his imagination. In *The Rape of the Daughters of Leucippus* (Plate V) he tells the story of the twins Castor and Pollux who were notorious for their equestrian skill. They kidnapped the two sisters Phoebe and Hilaria, who were the daughters of the Priest Leucippus. Idus and Lynceus, the fiancés of the girls, came to their rescue. A fight followed, between the girl's suitors and the twins and Castor was killed in the battle. Zeus intervened and allowed Pollux to die, too. The twins were placed among the stars and the constellation of Gemini came into being.

Rubens' approach to mythology was very similar to that of the young Bernini, who was working in Italy. They both used the Baroque techniques of synthesizing light, color, and movement to create an emotional reaction in the viewer. Bernini also had shown a concern in his mythological representations with the expression of sexual desire, and he had experimented with conveying movement by painting wind blown drapery.

Another function of the narrative style of painting was to retell history. *The Rape of the Sabines* (Plates LVI and LVII) takes on epic dimensions. Romulus, the founder of Rome attracted the first settlers by offering asylum to runaway slaves and criminals. They came to Rome empty-handed. In order to perpetuate Roman civilization, the refugees needed wives. Romulus devised a plan whereby he held a festival in honor of the god Consus. He invited the neighboring Latins and the Sabines to participate in the celebration. Then, at his signal, the Romans attacked their guests and abducted the young women to serve as their wives. Rubens was such a master of visual narrative that in this single painting he captured the gusto of the festivities, the gore of the battle and the exuberant triumph of the Romans at the success of their ploy. The entire story is in this one scene.

When Marie de Medicis, Queen of France, wished to decorate the Luxembourg Palace, which she had built, she was advised by her court to commission Rubens to undertake this task. According to the custom of the time, the subject of the pictures for the gallery was to be her history. This was the first time that Rubens' represented contemporary history. The Queen decided which events of her life she wanted painted. Marie de Medicis was the daughter of Francesco de Medicis Grand Duke of Tuscany. She was raised in isolation and led a lonely childhood. She had been unhappily married to King Henry IV of France: he had wooed her most ardently before the wedding, but that turned out to be only a political gesture. After he was assassinated, Marie tried unsuccessfully to govern France. She was so attached to her throne that she was constantly plotting even against her own son, Louis XIII, in order to hold on to her regency, and this eventually led to her exile at Blois. She escaped from Blois in 1619, which Rubens depicted in *The Escape from Blois* (Plate XLV). In April of that year, after a reconciliation was negotiated with her son, portrayed in *The Treaty of Angoulême* (Plate XLI), she returned to France. She was finally expelled from France in 1630 after Richelieu maneuvered her downfall. Rubens's genius was expressed by taking these rather uninteresting and often politically sensitive events and transforming them into masterpieces.

The twenty-four paintings of the Medici Gallery, *The Life of Marie de Medicis* (Plates VI through XLV), sequentially tell a story. Rubens strongly upheld the divine right of the monarchy. The gallery expressed the concept of the divinity of kings just at the time when it was becoming a popular idea. The premise was that a king or queen was not an ordinary human being beset by mortal limitations but rather an instrument of an Eternal Will which brought together in one person the immortal and transcendental laws to channel earthly destiny.

Bending Nude of a Man -
Paris, Musée du Louvre, Cabinet des Dessins

The heroine was a key ideal in the Queen's time. She wished to be portrayed as nothing less than heroic. In her contract with Rubens, drawn up under the guidance of Richelieu, it was specified that he was to portray the heroic deeds of the Queen. Rubens embellished the truth to make it fill that aim. He portrayed extraordinary adventures, noble deeds, fearless undertakings – thereby immortalizing the Queen's history with grandeur and sublimity.

Before Rubens returned to Antwerp to execute the paintings, fifteen subjects were agreed upon. They were: the Birth of the Queen, her Education, the Presentation of the Portrait, the Wedding by Proxy, Landing at Marseilles, the Wedding Festival at Lyons, the Birth of the Dauphin, the Coronation, the King's Death, the Regency, the Taking of Juliers, the Prosperity of the Regency, the Council of the Gods, the Marriage of Louis XIII, the Marriage of the Queen of Spain, and Delivering over the Government to the King. Later, four additional subjects were added, including *The Escape from Blois* and *The Treaty of Angoulême.* Rubens compared the Queen's birth to the Nativity. He used gods and goddesses to supervise her education. He alluded to her often as a goddess. Thus, the mythological and allegorical representations add interest to an otherwise dull and unglorified regency.

The Queen was amply satisfied with the completed gallery of paintings, which Rubens finished in only four years, rather than the ten or more years it would have taken any other painter. Throughout the canvases, Rubens used strong, dynamic colors with a gray motif underlying them. The whole gallery seemed to be bathed in light, except for one or two canvases, the theme of which necessitated the use of a more somber tone. Yellows and reds were used in full intensity, and, although Rubens did not like the color, blue was also used frequently because it was one of the colors of France.

For years after the Queen's final exile the gallery was all but forgotten. It was rediscovered in the eighteenth century by artists such as Delacroi and Cézanne. Delacroix devoted a great deal of energy to the study of Rubens. One of his fondest dreams was to revive his art. Cézanne, as well as other 18th and 19th century French artists visited the gallery and made drawings from the Medici cycle, much as Rubens had done with the Italian masters during his stay at the Court of the Duke of Mantua.

A year after completing the Medici cycle in 1626, Rubens experienced a profound grief at the sudden death of his wife, Isabella Brant. She was a beautiful woman with whom he had

The Prophet Geremia, copied from Michelangelo - Paris, Musée du Louvre

lived happily for fifteen years. He had painted the two of them together in *Rubens and His Wife Isabella in The Honeysuckle Bower* (Plate II).

Rubens was a family man, very much a devoted to his wife and their three children. After her death, in a letter to a close friend, Rubens eulogized his wife as a fine and noble woman who had given him much joy and sweetness. He spoke of her as an intelligent and sensitive person, a rare woman, whom he felt honored to have known. His sadness was so deep that he left his home and his studio in Antwerp, so that he could put behind the objects and places that reminded him of her.

Rubens always had an interest in the politics of Europe. Several times before, he had carried out informal diplomatic missions.

During his visit to the court of Marie de Medicis, the Archduchess Isabella of Flanders had secretly asked Rubens to determine the feeling of France concerning the reconciliation between the Catholic and Protestant factions in the Low Countries. Then, in 1626, just at the time Rubens decided to travel, civil conflict erupted in France. The Duke of Buckingham was straining already troubled relations between England and France by leading English troops to the support of the French Huguenots in their struggle with the Catholic monarchy. The regent of the Catholic Low Countries, who was officially an ally of France, wanted peace with England, but for this there was need of an understanding with Spain, the virtual ruler of Flanders. In this delicate situation, Rubens was sent to carry out negotiations, and he was instrumental in the eventual reconciliation of Spain and England. He spent the next four years primarily as a diplomat; infact, his paintings became merely a cloak for his real missions. During his years of diplomacy, he spent some time in Spain, where he met Velasquez and had the opportunity to study Spanish painting. By 1630, tired of traveling and somewhat politically disillusioned, Rubens returned to his home and his three children in Antwerp.

A new phase in his life began with his second marriage, in 1630, to sixteen-year old Helena Fourment, whom he had known since she was a young child. He was enamoured of her beauty, and she became the most frequently recurring figure in his later works.

Deposition - Amsterdam, Rijksmuseum

9

She became the heroine of his mythological works, and she was also painted several times as herself.

It was the custom with the Flemings to spend the summer months in the country, and, as Rubens grew older, he spent more and more time at his country estate.

Though in his earlier works he had hired specialists to do the landscape details, he now began to take a greater interest in painting landscapes himself. At that time, the Dutch landscape painters stressed the strong contrasts between the ethereal sky and the solid earth, but Rubens abandoned all dogma and painted his landscapes spontaneously, as a harmony between heaven and earth. He often included some sign of man's hand on earth, whether it was a bridge or people returning from work, as in *Return from the Fields* (Plate LXI). In Rubens's landscape paintings, one achieves the illusion of being out of doors. It was not until the nineteenth century that landscape painting in general reached the stage of naturalism at which he had already arrived in these late works.

Rubens' strong interest in the narrative is seen even in his landscapes. He uses the story of Philemon and Baucis, told by Ovid in *Metamorphosis, Book 8*, as an excuse to paint a magnificent storm landscape. When Jupiter and Mercury visited the earth in disguise they were refused food and shelter everywhere they went. Finally, an elderly couple, Philemon and Baucis, offered them hospitality. It wasn't much, for they were very poor, but they gave the gods everything they had. The gods punished the inhospitable citizens of the country with a terrible flood. As a reward, Philemon and Baucis, along with their modest cottage, were saved from the devastating disaster. Rubens used the theme of violence in nature, here, rather than his usual motif of human energy exerted upon and interacting with nature. His technical proficiency renders his canvas a showcase of color and form.

Rubens is an artist who impresses his viewers visually rather than intellectually. His paintings are not profound philosophical statements. His earlier works have a dramatic variation from light to dark that creates a sensual intensity. His light is composed of clear and delicate tints. His shadows, in contrast, are painted with very hot colors. In his later works, he abandons some of his former dramatic coloring. His objects become softer, often merging with the background in the distance. His palette becomes more versatile and he uses a wider variation of tones and hues. In his final years of painting, emotions more than ever became the major element in his works. *The Rape of the Sabines* is at once humorous, lyrical, violent, and sensual. He captured the tender feelings of a mother for her child, as well as his personal emotions for his wife and son in *Helena Fourment with Her Son* (Plate XLVIII). There is life in the painting: one never feels the fixed pose of the model, because even in this static scene there are suggestions of movement. He paints light in and around the subject, lifting it by suggesting air flowing around it and thus preventing it from being lost in the background.

Throughout his final illness, although he was progressively weakening, Rubens continued to paint. He died on May 20, 1640, leaving a voluminous number of paintings, estimated from 1,200 to 1,500. Rubens was a man of action with many diversified activities. He was content as a family man, influential as a diplomat and brilliant as an artist. His *Self-Portrait* (Plate XLIII) painted shortly before his death tells us something about the way he saw himself. He is present in many of his compositions at the request of a patron. However, he never painted himself as an artist. He has a sword at his side, an indication of his rank, and one of his hands is gloved in the manner of a fine gentleman – this was a fashionable gesture he adopted from Titian's male portraits. Shortly after his death, the School at Antwerp, which he had originated, closed. His paintings, however, were to have an endless influence. He had laid the foundation for English art; his most famous pupil, Van Dyke, aiding in this. Future generations of artists throughout Europe were to look back at his works, not to learn what to paint, but to emulate his genius in harmonizing colors and his techniques for applying them to canvas. Rubens, the artist and the diplomat, considered the whole world his native land, and his art and his widespread influence demonstrate the verity of that belief.

XV - The Triumph at Juliers, thirteenth painting in the Life of Marie de Medicis - *On september 1, 1610, immediately following the death of Henry IV, the queen regent returned Juliers to the hands of the Protestants, fulfilling the late king's promises. Above her are Victory, and Fame, who heralds her name. The woman with the lion, behind her, represents Force and Generosity.*

XVI - The Entry into Lyons, seventh painting in the Life of Marie de Medicis - *Marie awaited the king's arrival for a week in Lyons before their marriage took place there on November 11, 1600. In this painting, the king and queen represent Jupiter and Juno.*

XVII - The Entry into Lyons, detail of Plate XVI - *This is the view of the city of Lyons that appears in the distant corner of the painting. Landscapes were considered a very specialized type of painting, and it was therefore customary to have a specialist paint them in to larger works. No doubt, however, Rubens put the finishing touches on this one.*

XVIII - The Entry into Lyons, detail of Plate XVI - *The woman in the chariot represents the city of Lyons, and, on close examination, one sees that her crown is actually a miniature city. The two cupids, mounted on the lions, admire the new couple and celebrate their magnificence.*

XIX - Studies for The Entry into Lyons - *Rubens sketched these lions in various attitudes. He always strove to have movement in his work, rather than stiff, classical postures. Here he has created several views of a lion's behavior. He used the upper two lions in the final painting.*

XX - The Debarkation at Marseilles, sixth painting in The Life of Marie de Medicis - *The queen is shown arriving in Marseilles on November 3, 1600. The gestures, drapery, and colors combine to capture the excitement and commotion of the event. Rubens often used incandescent reds to add vitality to his paintings.*

XXI - The Debarkation at Marseilles, detail of Plate XX - *Neptune and Triton are accompanied by three sirens and a sea god. They have escorted the queen to the city of Marseilles. The sirens' flesh is infused with reflections of blue from the water. The movements are so masterfully illustrated that one feels this scene is only momentarily frozen.*

XXII - The Debarkation at Marseilles, detail of Plate XX - *Rubens's genius for narrative painting is evident here. Every detail of the story is thought out and recorded to give the allegory reality. In the smoke of a cannon shot from the gallery, Fame soars up and announces the queen's arrival with her trumpet.*

XXIII - The Debarkation at Marseilles, detail of Plate XX - *This fully armed knight wears a coat of banded mail with a Maltese cross on his tabord. Near him are oarsmen. The metal of the knight's suit looks cold and hard to the touch, the oarsmen look muscular and sweaty more evidence that Rubens was a master in depicting the sensual.*

XXIV and XXV - The Debarkation at Marseilles, detail of Plate XX - *The queen, majestic in her splendor, is greeted by France, the woman dressed in a blue cape emblazoned with gold fleurs-delis. The other woman who greets her, wearing a crown of towers, represents the city of Marseilles.*

XXVI - The Consignment of the Regency, ninth painting in The Life of Marie de Medicis - *On March 20, 1610, Henry IV departed for the war in Germany. Before leaving, he entrusted the queen with the government of the kingdom. The globe, decorated with lilies, is a symbol of power. The young dauphin is beneath it, his gaze up on the symbol of rule.*

XXVII - The Birth of the Dauphin, eighth painting in The Life of Marie de Medicis - *Apollo is seen riding his chariot across the sky, announcing the morning birth of Louis XIII on September 27, 1601. Justice holds the baby prince. The five newborns in the horn of plenty represents the number of children the king and queen would eventually have.*

XXVIII and XXIX - The Birth of the Dauphin, detail of Plate XXVII - *Rubens's study of antique sculpture is evident in this painting. The queen's relaxed pose and the classical position of her resting arm are reminiscent of a Roman statue. In her facial expression of tenderness toward the dauphin, we see the most touching appearance in all of the paintings done for the gallery.*

XXX and XXXI - Detail from The Felicity of the Regency, fifteenth painting in the Life of Marie de Medicis - *The full painting shows the queen seated on the throne of justice. Here, her hand is visible on the left, holding a scepter on a globe, a symbol of ruling power. This painting illustrates the queen's maintenance of power even after the dauphin had reached his majority. The two figures here represent Love and Abundance.*

XXXII - Sketch for The Coronation of the Queen, tenth painting in The Life of Marie de Medicis - Alte Pinakothek, Munich - *Rubens always made preliminary sketches in paint, and this is the second drawing of such a series. The final painting includes facets from each of his sketches.*

XXXIII - The Coronation of the Queen, detail - *Two genii shower gold coins on the queen. It was the custom, at great solemnities, to fling coins in great numbers after mass was said, and coins of gold and silver bearing a bust of the queen had been made for this occasion.*

XXXIV and XXXV - The Coronation of the Queen, detail - *The queen is on her knees receiving the crown from Cardinal de Joyeuse. The dauphin, dressed in white, and his sister, the princess, are beside her. The ceremony was grande and opulent.*

XXXVI and XXXVII - The Coronation of the Queen, detail - *Several princesses attend the queen. The attention to accurate rendition of costume was of vital importance in the seventeenth century. The faces of Rubens's women were often criticized for looking too much alike.*

XXXVIII - The Coronation of the Queen, detail - *The history in this painting, which actually represents the queen's Coronation as regent, is unembellished and very accurate. Princes and lords, many of whom could be identified by name in the painting, attended the ceremony. The Coronation was given a prominent position in the gallery to emphasize the importance as far as Marie de Medicis was concerned, its subject.*

XXXIX - The Coronation of the Queen, detail - *These two figures add brilliance to an otherwise dark painting. Here we have, two Rubens hallmarks the fiery reds and the sweeping drapery. Notice how the light from the candles casts its glow on the columns and figures.*

XL - The Exchange of the Princesses, sixteenth painting in The Life of Marie de Medicis - *On November 9, 1615, a double wedding took place between Anne of Austria and King Louis XIII, and Isabelle of France and King Philip IV of Spain. Originally, Rubens had planned a series of paintings to portray the double matrimony, but only this one was made.*

XLI - The Treaty of Angoulême, eighteenth painting in The Life of Marie de Medicis - *This painting also has the title, The Reconciliation of Marie de Medicis with Her Son, an event that took place April 30, 1619. Mercury descends from heaven and brings the olive branch as a sign of peace between the queen and her son.*

XLII - The Treaty of Angoulême, detail of Plate XLI - *This is the face of Cardinal de Guise, who stands next to the queen. He was instrumental in negotiating the reconciliation between the queen and her son. Rubens captured the solemn nature of the event in the face of the Cardinal.*

XLIII - The Treaty of Angoulême, detail of Plate XLI - *Mercury is the symbol of peace in this painting. He brings the olive branch to the queen. His status as a divine being is evident from the different way in which Rubens painted his form, his flesh is more delicate than that of the mortals.*

XLIV - Sketch for The Flight from Paris - 1621-1625 - Alte Pinakothek, Munich - *A final painting was never made from this sketch. The politics in The Flight were full of negative allusions and would have made for an indelicate situation. The theme is of a struggle between innocence and falsehood and it was feared that the monsters of falsehood that appear above the queen's head might be mistaken as personal rather than allegorical representations.*

XLV - The Escape from Blois, seventeenth painting in The Life of Marie de Medicis - *This painting shows the queen's escape from Blois on the night of February 21-22, 1619. It was a difficult ordeal for her, but she wanted the subject included in the cycle. There are three sources of light in this painting: the light of the moon, the light from the torches, and the light of early dawn in the left background. Rubens handled this skillfully.*

XLVI and XLVII - Rubens with Helena Fourment in the Garden - 1631 - Alte Pinakothek, Munich - *Four years after the death of his first wife in 1626, Rubens married sixteen year old Helena Fourment. Here he is seen with his new wife in the garden of their home in Antwerp. The looser brush stroke seen here characterized his work after 1630.*

XLVIII - Helena Fourment with Her Son - 1634 - Alte Pinakothek, Munich - *Rubens in his later years painted many portraits of his family and also used them as models for mythological figures. The use of color in this painting is a most positive yet unusual attribute, which was later emulated by other artists.*

XLIX - Le Chapeau de Paille (Portrait of Susanna Fourment - 1625 - National Gallery, London - *There is some doubt about the identity of the subject, but it is thought by some to be Susanna Fourment, Helena's elder sister. The title, translated as The Straw Hat, is also confusing, as the hat in the painting seems to be made of felt.*

LVI and LVII - The Rape of the Sabines - 1635 - National Gallery, London - *Romulus, the founder of Rome, encouraged settlers by offering asylum to refugees. His new Romans needed wives, so he organized a festival and invited neighbours. The Romans later attacked their guests and stole their women. An this panel painting, the central Sabine is a portrait of Helena Fourment.*

L - The Holy Family - 1635 - Prado Museum, Madrid - *There is a striking similarity between this religious painting and Helena Fourment with Her Son (Plate XLVIII). The same models were used for both paintings, and the relationship portrayed, between mother and child, is universal.*

LVIII - Madonna and Child - Date uncertain - Prado Museum, Madrid - *In Rubens's last years, his paintings tended to be less dramatic. This tender scene is soft and fluid in both color and brush stroke. There is a tranquillity in this work not evident in his earliest paintings.*

LI - The Garden of Love, detail - 1635 - Prado Museum, Madrid - *This contemporary allegory was inspired by Titian. It captures the poetry of an elegant and pleasure-loving society. Rubens wrought out its sensual theme through his handling of paint and color. This work is considered one of his last great masterpieces.*

LIX - The Triumph of the Church - Date uncertain - Prado Museum, Madrid - *The Church is triumphant in battle. The angel on horseback carries Peter's keys, the symbol of the Church. The divine right of the papacy is symbolized by the Crown held over the head of the figure in the chariot, who personifies the Church.*

LII - The Countryside with Little Bridge - Date uncertain - The Hermitage, Leningrad - *It was the Flemish custom to rest in the country during the summer. Rubens used this time to paint landscapes. Here, his colors become liquid and his brush stroke acquires an increasing spontaneity.*

LX - Landscape with Philemon and Baucis - 1630-1632 - Kunsthistorisches Museum, Vienna - *This painting illustrates Ovid's tale of Philemon and Baucis, the elderly couple saved from the punishing flood by Mercury and Jupiter. They were saved because they were the only ones who had offered hospitality to the gods, despite their poverty. Rubens took advantage of this story to portray a landscape, in which we see the power of a great storm.*

LIII - A Lady-in-Waiting to the Infanta - Date uncertain - Graphische Sommlung Albertina, Vienna - *Rubens used simple people as his models. He was criticized because his faces lacked the acceptable classical character found in Roman sculpture. However, Rubens's contemporaries agreed that his faces were remarkably beautiful, and this one is particularly sensitive.*

LXI - Return from the Fields - 1635-1638 - Pitti Palace, Florence - *Rubens rarely painted a landscape without some evidence of man's presence. He felt that man's most important relationship with the earth was expressed by his working in the fields. This warm scene indicates that attitude.*

LIV - Head of the King, study for The Life of Marie de Medicis - Date uncertain, Anvers - *When Rubens was commissioned to paint the series, he did several sketches and drawings of the king and queen in Paris and then returned to his studio in Antwerp to work on the paintings. This sketch of Henry IV was used for several paintings.*

LXII - The Enslavement of the Mother - Date uncertain - Royal palace, Arazzo, Turin - *This painting has been badly damaged but it can be seen here how Rubens built up his paintings layer by layer. He used hot colors in the folds of his drapery. Normally shadows would have been cool colors. The figures in this work reflect the influence of Roman sculpture.*

LV - Abundance, study for The Life of Marie de Medicis - Museum Von Benningen, Rotterdam - *It was the custom of the Netherland school to take nature and to include it in a fictional scene. Rubens took this model and transformed her into Abundance for The Felicity of the Regency (Plates XXX and XXXI).*

LXIII - Self-portrait - 1638-1640 - Kunsthistorisches Museum, Vienna - *This was painted shortly before his death in 1640. It is one of the few portraits of the artist alone. Rubens often included himself in his paintings at the request of a patron, but he never painted himself as an artist. Here he is as Rubens the diplomat, with his sword, the symbol of his status, at his side.*

15

IV

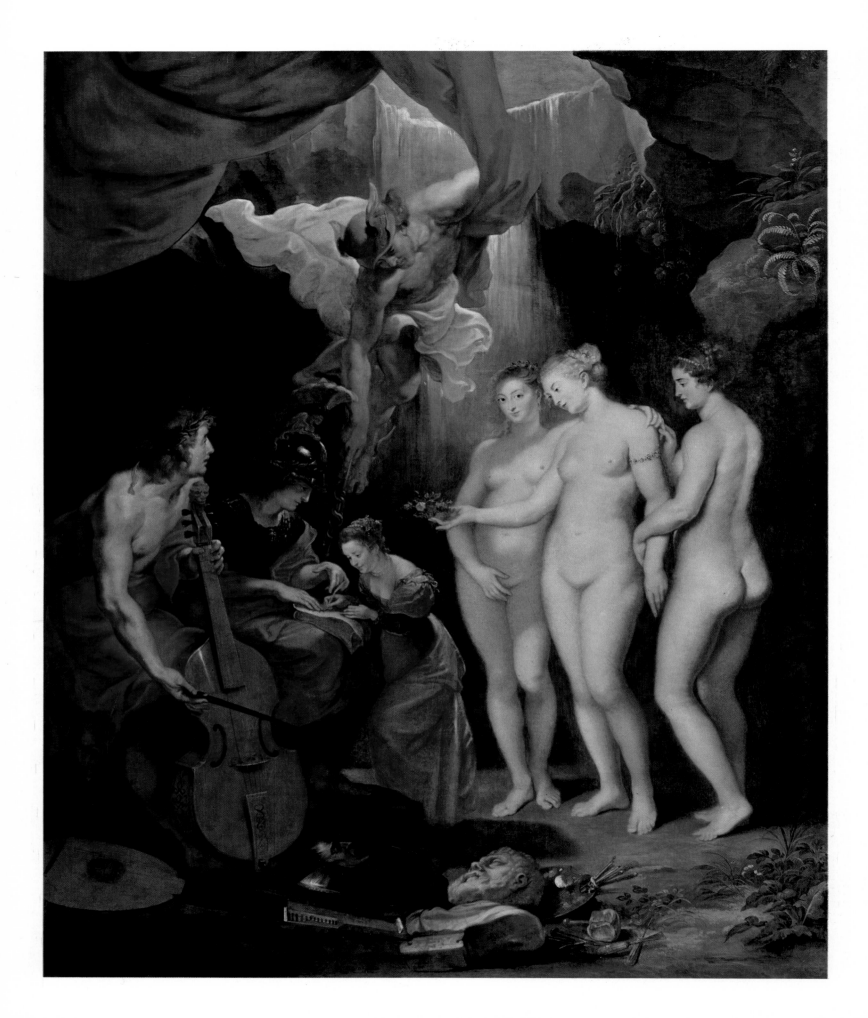

VII

VIII

XIV

XVII

XVIII

P. P. Rubens f⁺

XIX

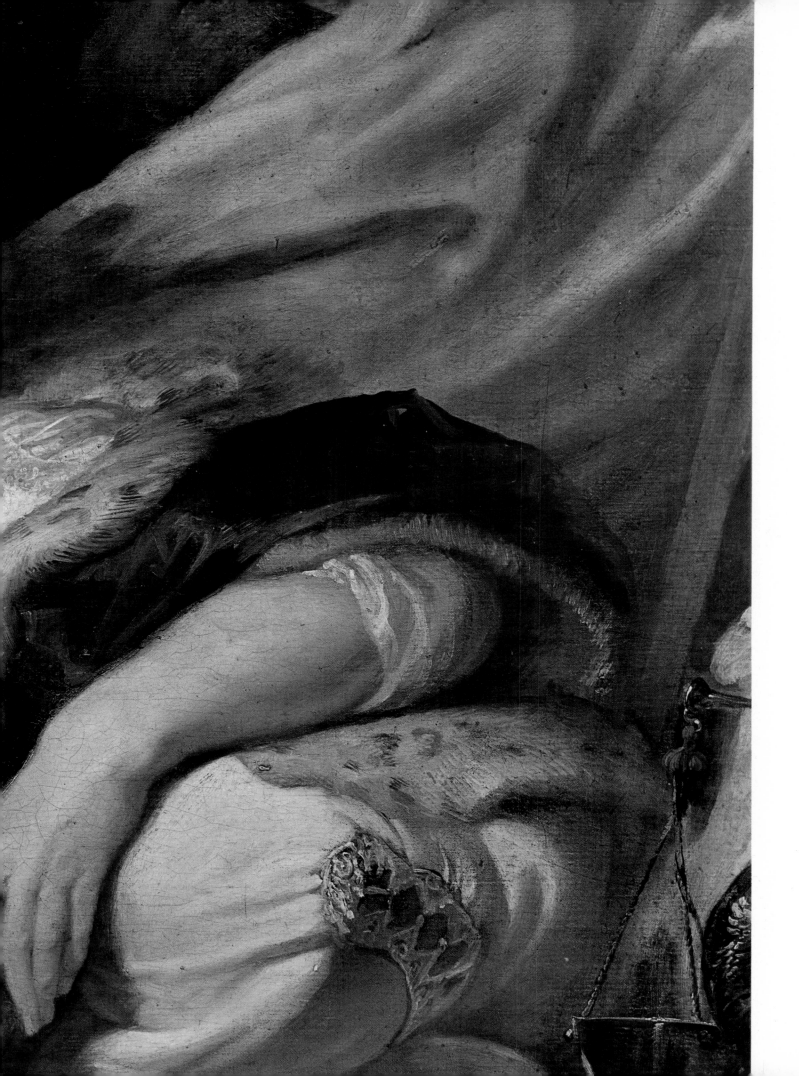

XXIX

XXXII

XXXVIII

LIV

LV

LVI

LVII

LVIII

LX

LXII

LXIII

Illustrations from the Picture Archives of Fabbri Editori, Milan
Printed in January 1980, at the graphic plant of Fabbri Editori - Milan, Italy